NAVAL
FIREPOWER

NAVAL
FIREPOWER

LINDSAY PEACOCK

a Salamander book

Published by Salamander Books Limited
LONDON • NEW YORK

A Salamander Book

Published by Salamander Books Ltd.
129-137 York Way,
London N7 9LG,
United Kingdom.

ISBN 0 86101 514 2

Distributed in the United Kingdom by:
Hodder and Stoughton Services,
PO Box 6,
Mill Road,
Dunton Green,
Sevenoaks.
Kent TN13 2XX

All correspondence concerning the content of this volume should be addressed to Salamander Books Ltd.

Designed by Paul Johnson
and the Maltings Partnership

Filmset by The Old Mill, London

Colour Reproduction by Scantrans Pte, Singapore, and Track Ltd, London

Printed and bound in Spain

Photo Credits
Jacket: (front and rear) US DoD, **Endpapers:** US DoD, **Page 1:** US DoD, **2/3:** UK MoD, **4/5:** US DoD, **6/7:** (left) US Navy, (right) US DoD, **8/9:** US DoD, **10/11:** (top left) SAAB, (rest) US DoD, **12/13:** US Navy, **14/15:** US DoD, **16/17:** (bottom right) McDD, (rest) US DoD, **18/19:** (bottom right) US DoD, (rest) McDD, **20/21:** US DoD, **22/23:** US DoD, **24/25:** US DoD, **26/27:** (left) Gary Kieffer/IDI, (top right) US DoD, (bottom right) Fred Sutter/IDI, **28/29:** (top right) US DoD, (rest) Grumman, **30/31:** R. Gaucher/DACT, **32/33:** US DoD, **34/35:** (top) Michael Anselmo/IDI, (bottom) McDD, **36/37:** US DoD, **38/39:** US DoD, **40/41:** US DoD, **42/43:** (clockwise from top left) Kirby Harrison/IDI, Mi Seitelman/IDI, F. Guenet/IDI, **44/45:** (Left) US DoD, (right) Lockheed, **46/47:** McDD, **48/49:** (left) Martin Marietta, (right) US DoD, **50/51:** US DoD, **52/53:** US Navy, **54/55:** US DoD, **56/57:** US DoD, **58/59:** Westland Helicopter, **60/61:** (left) Shorts, (right) UK MoD, **62/63:** (bottom right) Plessey Marine, (rest) UK MoD, **64/65:** (top right) Breda, (bottom right) Sistel, (rest) Italian MoD, **66/67:** (top left) US Navy, (rest) US DoD, **68/69:** US DoD, **70/71:** US DoD, **72/73:** (top right) US Navy, (bottom right) Goodyear Aerospace, (rest) US DoD, **74/75:** UK MoD, **76/77:** UK MoD, **78/79:** UK MoD, **80/81:** (top left) UK MoD, (rest) US DoD, **82/83:** (top left) Dutch MoD, (bottom left) HDW, (right) Thyssen, **84/85:** UK MoD, **86/87:** (clockwise from top left) US DoD, McDD, US Navy, **88/89:** US DoD, **90/91:** US DoD, **92/93:** (clockwise from top left) HSA, BAe, SAAB-Scania, **94/95:** (clockwise from top left) Kongsberg, Matra, Aerospatiale, **96/97:** US DoD, **98/99:** McDD, **100/101:** McDD, **102/103:** (left) Panavia, (right) MBB, **104/105:** US DoD, **106/107:** (top and bottom right) Aerospatiale, (rest) BAe, **108/109:** Matra, **110/111:** Kongsberg, **112/113:** IAI, **114/115:** US DoD, **116/117:** UK MoD, **118/119:** US DoD, **120/121:** (left) UK MoD, (rest) BAe, **122/123:** Selenia, **124/125:** GD, **126/127:** US DoD, **128/129:** (top and bottom left) HSA, (top and bottom right) Oerlikon, **130/131:** (right) US DoD, (rest) Jeremy Flack/API, **132/133:** US DoD, **134/135:** (clockwise from top left) Breda, Thomson-CSF, Oto-Melara, **136/137:** Oto-Melara, **138/139:** (top right) UK MoD, (rest) US DoD, **140/141:** US DoD, **142/143:** (clockwise from top left) Kaman, Westland, Italian MoD, **144/145:** (left) US DoD, (right) US Navy, **146/147:** (bottom left) Sikorsky, (rest) US DoD, **148/149:** (right) BAe, (rest) UK MoD, **150/151:** UK MoD, **152/153:** (left) UK MoD, (right) Westland, **154/155:** Aerospatiale, **156/157:** US DoD, **158:** US DoD.

Endpapers: Ohio class SSBN
Page 1: Aegis class cruiser and Standard SAM
2/3: Royal Navy Type 42 destroyer
4/5: Aegis class and Sea Sprite helicopter
6: 6-inch guns
7: Standard missile and USS Ticonderoga
8: USS Ticonderoga in heavy seas
9: Sea Sparrow missile launch
10: (top) Combat centre on Swedish Spica class; (bottom) Asroc missile/torpedo leaving box launcher
11: F-14 Tomcat on launch catapult

INTRODUCTION

WHETHER IT BE a Soviet Delta-class strategic submarine, a French Georges Leygues-class destroyer or an American Nimitz-class aircraft carrier, the warship of the modern era is hugely different from those that fought out the last great sea battles of World War II. Then, it was normal to enter into combat at relatively close range against a clearly visible enemy if one was to stand a reasonable chance of defeating an enemy force.

At that time there were definite pointers to the future and, in particular, to the desirability of being able to destroy an opponent at extreme range, secure in the knowledge that one was unlikely to come under threat of a counter-attack. Perhaps the single most important development of that conflict was the coming of age of the aircraft carrier as a weapon of war, carrier-borne air power permitting conclusive engagements to take place between widely separated naval task groups. Indeed, there were a number of conclusive encounters — most notably in the Pacific between the USA and Japan — in which crews embarked on opposing warships never actually saw their opponents.

More often than not, though, it was necessary to be able to see one's enemy before one could destroy him, most commonly by means of gunfire. In consequence, most surface combatants of that era were little more than gun platforms, relying on such weapons for both offense and defence. Today, after a period in which the missile was perceived as being "the only game in town" and the humble gun as little more than an anachronism,

the latter has to some extent come back into favour and most contemporary warships do have some form of gun armament in their offensive and defensive weapons systems.

Nevertheless, it cannot be denied that the nature of naval warfare has changed irrevocably and it is equally clear that sea battles of the future will for the most part be fought out at great range, by opponents who view each other as nothing more than blips on a radar display and with missiles being the main weapons employed in any serious "exchange of views".

Increasing sophistication in terms of armament has been more than matched by improvements elsewhere and it is in these other areas that warships have undoubtedly experienced the greatest changes over the past few decades. Driven in part by the fantastic progress made in micro-miniaturisation and fuelled by the understandable desire to embody the latest technology, the warship of the eighties and nineties is a fearsomely complex and sophisticated entity.

It is also hugely expensive, which is one reason why most navies have contracted in size, for there are few nations with either the financial clout or the political will to spend the kind of money that the USA and the USSR have invested in sea power. Even there, though, it seems that retrenchment is very much in prospect in view of the warming relations that now exist between these two super-powers.

In theory, the adoption of new technology should result in significantly enhanced capabilities in the areas of attack, defence, detection or command and control. In reality, of course, many of the potential benefits may be negated by cost considerations, procurement policies often being at the mercy of limited budgets. The end result is that the ensuing warship may be nothing more than a compromise between that which is deemed to be most desirable and that which is most affordable.

"Cost versus capability" is an equation that has been with us for many years, with spending on defence ever being victim to "financial constipation" during times of peace. In the normal course of events, financial cheeseparing goes unnoticed (at least as far as the general public is concerned) and it takes something like the Falklands conflict to reveal the shortcomings of this policy.

Then, in the face of determined attacks by Argentinian pilots, it became grimly evident that British warship design had not devoted quite as much attention to safety factors as it might have done. By way of illustration, the inability to control the fire aboard HMS *Sheffield* was without doubt the main cause of that vessel's loss after she was struck by an AM.39 Exocet anti-shipping missile fired from a Dassault-Breguet Super Etendard of Argentina's Naval Air Arm.

Subsequent reappraisal of design and the deletion of highly inflammable materials such as plastic will do much to reduce the hazards posed by fire and

smoke but the situation with regard to command and control is perhaps less easy to resolve.

In this context, it is clear that "high-tech gizmos" are vulnerable to a well-aimed weapon or even the hard-to-foresee chance hit in a key area. It is easy to appreciate the military's desire to take advantage of the benefits of technology but there do appear to be all-too-many instances where these benefits have only been achieved at the cost of economies in other areas with the result that the new systems are themselves sadly lacking in protection. Knock out the computer and the chances are that you will also knock

out a warship's ability to operate by rendering it electronically "blind" and, in consequence, virtually unable to defend itself, let alone make any valid contribution to the prosecution of war at sea.

Increased levels of sophistication have been accompanied by the need for greater skill on the part of those whose job it is to crew the modern warship and this is one area where training has perhaps been deficient. Certainly, when it comes to interpreting the flood of information that is now available on the evolving tactical situation, there is clear evidence to support the contention that the modern sailor has too much data at his fingertips

and is becoming less able to reach the correct conclusions.

That certainly seems to have been the case aboard the USS *Vincennes* and had quite tragic consequences for those unfortunate enough to be flying in the Iran Air Airbus which was erroneously perceived to present a threat to the US warship. In fairness, though, it must be emphasised that this is by no means a problem unique to the US Navy although it is perhaps more apparent there by virtue of the sheer size of the service and its relative openness when it comes to discussing military matters.

Quite how one can go about dealing

with the thorny question of human fallibility is perhaps the most important problem facing contemporary naval powers. Some have suggested that greater use could be made of computers but that is perhaps too easy an answer. There are others who question the wisdom of increasing still more the degree of dependence that is placed on this most complex of human servants, arguing that the processes of command and control are aspects that are just too important to be entrusted to mere machines.

Human fallibility may from time to time result in tragic errors but man does at least have the ability to reason, unlike

computers which merely react to electrical stimuli. Perhaps the best answer is to allocate more of the budget to realistic training and to make much greater use of simulation exercises.

Regardless of one's views on such arcane matters as these, there can be no doubt that contemporary warships are imposing vessels in their own right and this volume is devoted to providing some insight into the quite awesome array of firepower that is now available.

This volume examines most classes of warship — ranging from mighty battle-ships to the much smaller frigates and destroyers, through strategic and attack submarines to aircraft carriers and amphibious assault ships. In the pages that follow are examples of the often bewildering array of armament that presently constitutes the devastatingly powerful arsenal at the disposal of the modern Admiral of the Fleet.

Fittingly, the personnel who work, eat and sleep aboard these disparate vessels are not overlooked, for, when all is said and done, it is still up to man to decide when and, indeed, if the machinery at his disposal is put to the use for which it was intended. Those uses encompass virtually everything from fishery protection patrols, surface combat, anti-submarine warfare through surgical strike by carrier-borne air power, to nuclear devastation. In one form or another, the contemporary warship is more than able to fulfil the mission demanded of it, whether as a peacetime deterrent or in an actual "hot" war. It is hoped that this volume will provide the reader with a feel for the subject matter it examines and encourage further exploration of matters maritime.

There are few scenes that can compare with the sight of a naval Task Force under way. A typical US Navy Battle Group is shown here, with the aircraft carrier at the core of an imposing collection of surface vessels. Also visible are a battleship ahead of the carrier, three guided missile cruisers and an assortment of frigates and destroyers which serve as the protective screen. Finally, a handful of support craft such as fuel and aummunition store ships are in evidence, these being essential adjuncts to a Task Force's ability to wage effective war at sea.

The ultimate in naval gun power — the 16-inch battery of USS Iowa. The sheer visual effect of such a battleship broadside is unmatched by any other naval weapon, with the huge sheets of flame reflected in the sea's surface. The aerial view (below) also shows the eight box launchers for Tomahawk cruise missiles and the quad launcher units for Harpoon.

Following the advent of the aircraft carrier, the mighty battleship was long perceived as an anachronism and it was only fairly recently that it again found favour with the US Navy which restored a few Iowa class vessels to service during the 1980s. Now, harsh economies in defence spending seem set to curtail their careers and these studies of the USS *New Jersey* at sea (left) and firing Tomahawk (right) and Harpoon (below) might well mark the battleship's swan-song, although this has been said before.

The BGM-109 Tomahawk cruise missile (right) is available in surface and sub-surface launched versions, options on offer including at least four naval models with different warhead types. Nuclear and conventional warheads exist for land attack and there is a derivative that can dispense submunitions as well as one for anti-ship attacks.

One of the more unusual items of equipment used by the recently renovated Iowa class battleships is the Israeli Pioneer drone, this remotely piloted vehicle being used to monitor gunfire as well as performing reconnaissance tasks. These pictures show Pioneer at the moment of launching (left and above) and about to hit a capture net at the end of a mission (right). The above view also shows the transparent dome covering the electro-optics sensor package. Operations are invariably conducted from the helicopter platform at the stern and all four US battleships are capable of employing this system.

The second Nimitz class "supercarrier" to enter service, the USS *Eisenhower* is shown here cruising with elements of the embarked Air Wing seemingly scattered in haphazard fashion around her massive flight deck.

Entering service during the Vietnam war, Vought's Corsair was the primary light attack aircraft aboard the US Navy's large fleet of carriers until well into the 1980s when it began to be replaced by the multi-role McDonnell Douglas F/A-18 Hornet. Now very much in decline, the definitive Corsair version was the A-7E with the Spey turbofan engine and a trio of FLIR-equipped machines are portrayed here as they fly over the USS *Eisenhower*.

With regard to sea power, few countries can match the might of the United States and none come anywhere near in terms of carrier-borne air power. With a fully-laden displacement that exceeds 91,000 tons, the USS *Carl Vinson* (right) is a typical example of the Nimitz class of aircraft carrier. This nuclear-powered warship can accommodate an Air Wing with up to 90 aircraft able to perform a multiplicity of missions. Strike against land and sea targets is one such task and this has been ably satisfied by both the Grumman A-6E Intruder and Vought A-7E Corsair for many years. Some representatives of these most potent warplanes are readied for launch in company with an electronic warfare-dedicated EA-6B Prowler (left) while an F-14 Tomcat crew is depicted strapping in (right, below) as they prepare for a combat air patrol in defence of the carrier and other elements of the Task Force.

The Grumman
Intruder/Prowler family is an
integral part of the modern
Carrier Air Wing and both
types would almost certainly
feature in any strike mission
staged from a US Navy
aircraft carrier. The four-seat
Prowler (left) is designed for
the electronic warfare role and
uses the sophisticated
AN/ALQ-99 tactical jamming
system to blind enemy
defensive radars while the two-
seat Intruder (above and right)
operates solely in the attack
role and has the ability to
deliver a wide-ranging array of
weaponry.

Responsible for inflicting a considerable amount of damage on Royal Navy warships during the 1982 Falklands War, the Super Etendard serves in the strike role from French Navy aircraft carriers and is able to operate with the AM39 Exocet sea-skimming anti-ship missile as well as with more powerful nuclear weapons like the ASMP cruise missile. In service with the naval air arms of Argentina and France, the example shown here at the moment of launch is from the latter country.

A member of the deck crew looks on almost disinterestedly as, its shape blurred by speed, a Grumman F-14A Tomcat thunders past a tractor and an idle Intruder during recovery on a US Navy carrier. Sometimes described as nothing more than a "well controlled crash", the act of bringing an aircraft safely aboard calls for great skill on the part of the pilot who must also be superbly fit to tolerate the physical effects inherent in repeated jarring impacts and decelerations.

Many Hornet pilots and operators claim that this versatile multi-role aircraft is in effect a "one-plane airforce". While this may be somewhat of an exaggeration, it has provided new levels of capability to the US Navy and Marine Cops.

The difficulties of operating aircraft and helicopters from ships at sea are compounded by a lack of space as these pictures clearly reveal. The above view is of hangar deck accommodation on one of the US Navy's "supercarriers" as aircraft are loaded while the view at right depicts a mechanic performing maintenance on an SH-60B aboard a US frigate.

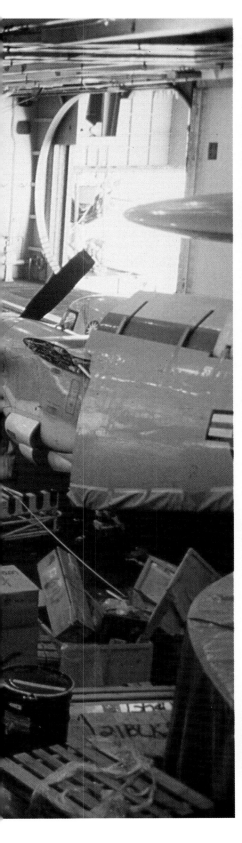

Aircraft carriers are as much above people as machinery and this selection shows a few of them going about their duties on the flight deck. The view above depicts an A-7E Corsair pilot conferring with members of a catapult crew. Elsewhere, a fuelling team tops up tanks on a Hornet (top right) and a screwdriver-wielding engineer "tweaks" the engine assembly of a Sikorsky SH-3 Sea King.

The very nature of flight operations at sea makes for memorable photographic images such as that above showing an A-7E Corsair moments before snagging an arrester wire as a blood-red sun sinks towards the horizon. Carriers also provide many opportunities to the imaginative photographer, epitomised here by a fine study of the island structure of the USS *Enterprise*.

Moody and magnificent, the aircraft carrier is a highly atmospheric workplace and an often hazardous one. Flight operations from ships at sea allow only minimal room for error, whether it be on the part of aviators or deck crew. These pictures convey a little of that atmosphere and show a Grumman A-6E Intruder with hook dangling and speed brakes deployed as it makes a final approach to an arrested landing (above), a McDonnell Douglas F/A-18 Hornet leaving the flight deck of the USS *Constellation* (far right) and deck crew on a French carrier almost engulfed by the steam that is an ever-present facet of launch operations (right).

Less spectacular than their gun-toting and bomb-dropping counterparts, Lockheed's S-3A Viking (right) and Grumman's E-2C Hawkeye (above) still constitute integral elements of a fully-fledged Carrier Air Wing. No "Air Boss" in his right mind would be keen to deploy without them and the support that they offer in essential anti-submarine warfare and airborne early warning tasks.

(Previous page) Few capital ships possess anything approaching the degree of strike power to be found aboard an aircraft carrier. America's Navy ranks supreme as the World's major exponent of carrier-borne air power and is currently adding a new Nimitz-class vessel to its fleet every few years. The carrier seen here, with an F/A-18 Hornet heading skywards while others taxi forwards in anticipation of launching, is the USS *Coral Sea*. Laid down in the final stages of WWII, the *Coral Sea* has just been retired as an economy measure but the Intruders and Hornets which flew from its flight deck until recently undoubtedly made it a force to be reckoned with.

Designed primarily to counter saturation attacks by threats from the air, the Ticonderoga class guided-missile cruisers rank amongst the most potent warships in service with the US Navy. They tote a comprehensive armoury of weapons systems, being able to employ Standard, Harpoon, Asroc and Tomahawk missiles for defence and offence as well as more conventional weapons such as torpedoes, five-inch guns and the 20mm Vulcan/Phalanx rapid fire close-in system. These two views show examples of the Standard vertical launch SAM being salvoed from a Ticonderoga, which has the capability to control 22 missiles in flight. The heart of this impressive potential lies with the Aegis Combat System and one of the four SPY-1 planar arrays that feed data to the computer for processing and display to the crew is visible (far left) as are the aft vertical launch missile containers.

The US Navy's Spruance class destroyers possess a well balanced mix of offensive and defensive weapons, including a pair of five-inch guns, two Phalanx CIWS units, torpedoes and launchers for Asroc, Sea Sparrow and Harpoon missiles. Ongoing update programmes are providing compatibility with the Tomahawk cruise missile, which, in concert with other improvements, will enable the class to remain viable until well into the 21st century. Representatives depicted here consist of the lead ship, USS *Spruance* (left, top) and the USS *Oldendorf* (left) while a Tomahawk missile is seen as it accelerates away from one of the updated ships (above).

The Mk45 dual-purpose 5-inch
gun and the box launcher for
the Asroc anti-submarine
missile dominate the foredeck
in this fine study of the USS
John Young, one of a large
number of Spruance class
destroyers currently in service.

Over 50 Oliver Hazard Perry frigates have been completed for service with the US Navy and three of these, including the lead ship, are seen above in close order while the view at right shows the helicopter landing area of another ship of the class. Adjacent hangar accommodation exists for two SH-2F Seasprite or two SH-60B Seahawk helicopters. On the opposite page, personnel work with the Sperry Mk.92 fire control system which manages an armament array made up of surface-to-air and surface-to-surface missiles as well as torpedoes, an OTO Melara 76mm gun and the 20mm Vulcan Phalanx CIWS.

In widespread service with the USA, Australia and Spain, the Oliver Hazard Perry class of frigate is portrayed here by the USS *Crommelin* (above) and the USS *Ford* (left), each having an identical array of armament comprising Standard and Harpoon missiles, torpedo tubes, the Phalanx CIWS and an OTO Melara 76mm dual purpose gun, backed up by an impressive and sophisticated set of electronic "goodies".

One of the most successful warships to be designed and built by the United Kingdom in the post-war era has been the Leander class frigate. In production for a decade, some 23 vessels of this type were completed for the Royal Navy while a further 20 were sold to Australia, Chile, Holland, India and New Zealand. Shown here kicking up the spray as it ploughs its way through a moderate sea is HMS *Minerva,* which, like its sisters, has a single Lynx helicopter to boost its anti-submarine warfare potential.

Eight examples of the Type 21 Amazon class of frigate were produced for service with the Royal Navy and seven of them saw combat in the Falklands where two members — *Antelope* and *Ardent* — were sunk. HMS *Ambuscade* (above) survived and one element of its suite of armament is Shorts' Seacat surface-to-air missile (left) with a range of about four miles.

Progressive refinement of the Type 42 destroyer over more than ten years of production has seen these ships grow in size to accommodate new equipment. Some examples that serve with Britain's Royal Navy are being given extra armament to counter threats from the air similar to that responsible for the destruction of two members of the Sheffield class during the battle for the Falklands. The attractive lines of the Type 42 are displayed by HMS *Edinburgh* (right) with other facets including the Vickers 4.5in dual-purpose automatic gun (below) and the three-man operators' console associated with the Plessey Type 2016 sonar (below right) fitted to later members of this class.

Although it doesn't possess a large fleet, Italy's maritime tradition can be traced back several hundred years and is still very much alive as this selection confirms. Clockwise from the left, these pictures depict a Sparviero class hydrofoil at speed as it fires an Otomat missile, a Breda 40mm twin anti-aircraft guns system, a Sea Killer Mk.2 anti-ship missile being launched and the *Ardito*, one of a pair of Audace class destroyers in service with today's Navy. An elegant vessel, the armament package includes a brace of 127mm guns, Standard SAMs and torpedoes.

At the top end of the scale when it comes to destructive power are the nuclear-powered and nuclear-armed strategic submarines (SSBN) which serve with both of the superpowers. The latest US SSBN is the Ohio class (far right) which can carry 24 examples of the Trident missile (right and below), each of which is able to deliver as many as eight MIRVs (multiple independently targetable re-entry vehicles).

Development and deployment of submarine-launched variations of the Harpoon and Tomahawk missiles has greatly enhanced the offensive capabilities of the US Navy's nuclear-powered attack submarines which are now able to strike at targets on both land and sea. Launch of a Tomahawk is depicted on this page, the view on the right showing a weapon at the moment of boost motor ignition while that below is taken a few seconds later when the missile is well into its initial climb. A standard weapon on the big Los Angeles class, Tomahawk has also been retrospectively provided to older SSNs of the Sturgeon class, represented by the USS *Queenfish* at speed on the surface (far right).

The Los Angeles class attack submarines form a massive investment on the part of the USA. The 50 or so boats now in service are some of the most effective nuclear-powered hunter-killer submarines at sea, with a powerful range of armament options. On the opposite page, the USS *Oklahoma City* (top) and the USS *San Francisco* (bottom) are depicted running on the surface with the views on this page showing a Subroc missile emerging from the sea (left) and ratings striking down a conventional torpedo (above).

Modern submarines are now far more versatile when it comes to engaging surface targets, being able to employ a choice of weapons which includes the familiar but hugely improved torpedo as well as specialist anti-ship missiles. At left, crewmen on a British attack submarine of the Trafalgar class struggle to direct a Mk.24 Tigerfish wire-guided torpedo into the cramped stowage spaces below deck. Another boat of this type, HMS *Turbulent* is shown in the action of surfacing (right bottom) while a rating uses a practice weapon as he runs through the procedures that are involved in readying a Sub-Harpoon missile for firing from one of the boat's torpedo tubes (right, top).

Unique in that it is the only
nuclear-powered submarine yet
to have employed its sensors and
weaponry in anger, HMS
Conqueror was responsible for
sinking the Argentinian heavy
cruiser *Belgrano* during the 1982
Falklands War. Interestingly,
rather than use sophisticated
homing weapons *Conqueror*
fired a salvo of three wartime
vintage unguided Mk.8
torpedoes at its target, two of
which found their mark.

(Overleaf) The latest class of nuclear-powered submarine to see service with Britain's Royal Navy is the Trafalgar class. Represented here by HMS *Turbulent,* the Trafalgars can use Tigerfish torpedoes, Sub-Harpoon missiles and Sea Urchin or Stonefish mines.

Claustropobia sufferers are unlikely to ever feel at ease in the restricted spaces of a submarine but these crewmen all look contented enough as they go about their tasks. In the picture above, a helmsman steers his British boat while the view at left portrays a missile launch team at work at the control panel aboard a US Navy Ohio class SSBN. Lastly an American officer takes advantage of a lull in activity to catch up on some "book-learning" as he studies technical manuals in the sonar station of a Los Angeles attack submarine.

Conventionally-powered types of submarine are by no means defunct as this selection of pictures shows. At left is a member of the Dutch Zwaardvis class and below is an example of the highly-successful German-designed Type 209 produced in India for service with that nation's Navy. Right is another German-designed boat, this TR1700 submarine being one of two that were supplied to Argentina which is to make three more in its own yards. In each case, torpedoes form the sole armament, the Type 209, for instance, being able to carry eight in bow tubes along with up to six reloads.

(Overleaf) The transfer of supplies when under way is a routine aspect of operations with navies all round the world. In the Royal Navy, it is referred to as "replenishment at sea" and it is exemplified here by an Illustrious class carrier and the RFA vessel *Olmeda*.

Not for naught do the Marines make the proud claim "first to fight" for this service is usually in the vanguard when US military might goes into action. Amphibious warfare is their forté but capabilities don't end there, elements of this elite body fulfilling a variety of missions, some of which entail flying aircraft and helicopters from ships like the USS *Guam* (right). Aerial assets include V/STOL machines such as the Harrier and an extensive selection of helicopters which move troops and equipment in addition to undertaking fire support, resupply and liaison duties. Helicopters in service range in size from the handy UH-1N Iroquois through the fearsome AH-1W SeaCobra to the CH-46 Sea Knight and the massive CH-53 Sea/Super Stallion troop transporter.

When it comes to insertion of ground-based fighting forces, the US Marine Corps is adept at accomplishing this by either amphibious landing craft (far left) or by helicopter (left). The Corps assault capability certainly doesn't end there for it also has the potential to transfer exceedingly heavy and bulky armoured fighting vehicles from ship to shore, tanks and LVTP7s being depicted "on the beach" in the view above.

As well as more conventional types of landing craft, the US Navy employs the LCAC hovercraft in support of Marine Corps ground forces. These "surface effect" vessels offer a rapid method of moving troops, vehicles and supplies to shore. Large and noisy, they seem easily detectable and vulnerable to enemy fire but the Navy hopes that speed and surprise will provide sufficient protection.

When it comes to defence of coastal waters, small, fast patrol boats offer a number of advantages over far larger warships. Sweden has invested fairly heavily in this type of vessel, with the Spica II (above) carrying an impressive array of weaponry, including a 57mm dual-purpose gun and the RBS15 anti-ship missile, an example of, which is shown being launched (right). Another useful inshore defence weapon is the British surface launched Sea Skua (top right) which can be housed in box launchers and installed on any light naval craft.

Coastal defence is a mission that is traditionally linked with naval warfare and many navies do feature small, fast and well-armed vessels to undertake inshore sovereignty patrols. Putting a ship-based surface-to-surface missile on a land-based launcher is another way of defending coastal waters and each one of the weapons illustrated here could inflict heavy damage on a naval force. The infamous MM40 Exocet seen on launch (left) has already proven itself when launched from ships or aircraft. Above that, Norway's Penguin is shown in its neat mobile box launcher while a Matra Otomat emerges from a shroud of smoke and heads on its way to a distant target (above).

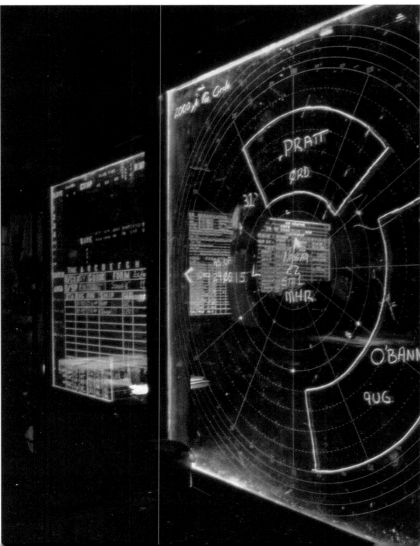

C³, or, to give it its full title, command, control and communications, is a vital and complex aspect of operations aboard the contemporary warship. In an era when the computer rules, the humble keyboard is an increasingly common sight and is shown in use by an electronic support measures operator as he monitors his visual display terminal (far left). Above, sailors manning the combat information centre of the destroyer USS *John Young* study radar data while the picture at left shows a more conventional area defence display using traditional china-graph inscriptions on perspex to indicate prime areas of interest.

Ship-launched versions of the Harpoon missile are shown in action here from a variety of US Navy vessels including one of the few extant battleships (below). One of the greatest bonus points of this type of weapon is that the simple tube launchers can be installed on virtually any warship in service and the US Navy has not been slow to recognise that fact, fitting Harpoon to most of the present fleet. Harpoon only needs a simple update of target position before launch as final homing is automatic.

The deadliest threat to a modern surface ship is the guided missile which can home on to its target from over 30 miles away. The versatile American Harpoon is one of the best systems in this class with air-, surface- and submarine-launched models all in service. Some idea of the devastating destructive power possessed by these missiles can be had from scrutiny of the picture above which shows a stricken US Navy frigate employed as a target for Harpoon trials with a live warhead.

Employed for maritime attack and reconnaissance missions, a Tornado strike aircraft of West Germany's Marineflieger (above) carries two Kormoran anti-ship missiles under its belly. Another "sea-skimmer", Kormoran's penetrative power is graphically illustrated in the picture on the right showing a test specimen at the moment of impact on a retired ship.

The destructive potential of the Tomahawk cruise missile is clear from these pictures which show yet another attack mode that may be employed by this versatile weapon, namely a vertical dive in the final phase of flight. Aiming point appears to be the cone that is visible in the left-hand view, with this and the rest of the building being damaged beyond repair in the ensuing warhead detonation.

Amongst the latest generation of weapons, sea-skimming anti-ship missiles are perhaps the most feared. Exocet and Sea Eagle are representative of these devices and both are illustrated here, the former being shown (above and below) at the moment of launch from a French Navy frigate of the D'Estienne D'Orves type while the latter is seen (left and right) being carried by a Sea King helicopter of the Fleet Air Arm and a Buccaneer S.2 of the Royal Air Force.

Yet another variation on the anti-shipping missile theme is the Italian Otomat, shown here at the moment of launch. Two solid-propellant rockets burn for just four seconds to propel Otomat from its tube before a single 400kg thrust Turbomeca Arbizon turbojet takes over. The latest version is able to engage targets at distances over 62 miles (100km).

Less well known than other weapons of its type, Norway's Penguin anti-ship missile is nonetheless a potent system and one that has demonstrated good reliability in service. Launched from ships or aircraft, Penguin uses infra-red terminal homing to give more positive identification among the islands and fjords of the Norwegian coastline. In this picture, a ship-launched Penguin is impelled skywards by the solid-fuelled rocket motor as it accelerates away from a frigate. Range is of the order of 19 to 25 miles (30 to 40km) and the Penguin warhead is a 120kg semi-armour piercing type.

Israel's armament industry is the source of much hardware for use by that nation's armed forces and it has evolved its own "sea-skimmer" in the form of the Gabriel missile which has been widely exported. The Gabriel began life in purely ship-launched form (above and above right) but continuing development has resulted in an air-launched version, seen (right) carried by an F-4E Phantom.

With the US Navy, the air defence function is in part allotted to the Standard surface-to-air missile, shown suspended on its firing rail (below) and in the process of launching from a vertical-launch cell on a Ticonderoga class cruiser (right).

With a range of the order of 50 miles (80km), the British Aerospace Sea Dart is now the Royal Navy's only long-range surface-to-air missile system. Sea Dart currently serves aboard a dozen Type 42 destroyers and all three of the Invincible class aircraft carriers, one of which is shown here firing an example of this weapon from the twin-launcher sited in the bow. Blooded in combat during the Falklands War, Sea Dart was responsible for the destruction of several enemy aircraft, including examples of the Canberra and Skyhawk.

One of the most widely used anti-aircraft weapons is the RIM-7 Sea Sparrow which forms the lethal element of the US Basic Point Defense Missile System. In service with most NATO navies, Sea Sparrow also plays a notable part in the layered defence of larger US warships such as aircraft carriers and amphibious assault vessels. Examples of Sea Sparrow are shown being fired from both types of vessel and the missiles are normally housed in four- or eight-round box launchers on rotating mounts.

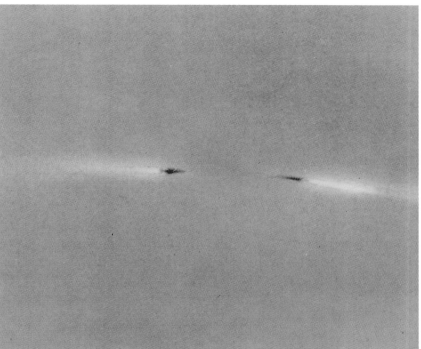

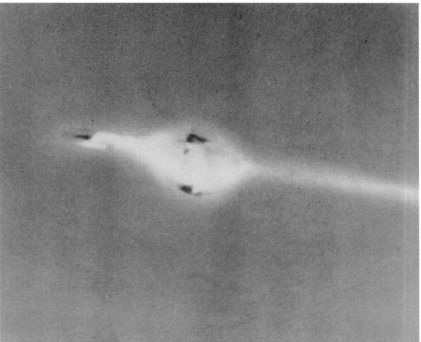

When it comes to the question of protection from aircraft or sea- skimming anti ship missiles, modern warships such as this Broadsword class frigate of the Royal Navy now rely mainly on missiles. Quick-reacting defensive systems have the potential to counter such threats at greater range than conventional guns. One such missile is Seawolf and a six-round launcher may be seen just ahead of the bridge of this ship while another is carried aft. Efforts to improve Seawolf continue, the vertical-launch version shown on a test firing above being designed to dispense with the weight of the standard launcher.

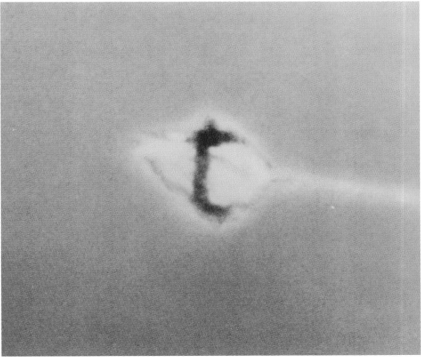

An Italian-built version of the Sea Sparrow surface-to-air missile, Aspide has met with considerable success and is now well established in service with at least fifteen navies throughout the world. Four- or eight-cell launchers are available as part of the Selenia Albatross package and the system is compatible with a variety of types of fire-control equipment, making it a popular choice for third- world nations.

Seen here moments after being fired from a 21-round EX-31 box launcher, the Rolling Airframe Missile results from a joint US and West German venture and is intended to augment existing anti-missile defence systems with both navies. Joint production should eventually result in nearly 7,000 missiles being built but it has yet to enter operational service.

One of the most widely used Close-In Weapons Systems is the Mk.15 Phalanx. Based on the hugely successful Vulcan M61A1 20mm six-barrel cannon, coupled to a radar-directed fire-control system, it is fully automatic and the associated magazine holds 1,000 depleted-uranium shells which are effective at ranges of 450 to 1,500 yards (400 to 1350m). Loading procedure is shown at left while the view at right is of a test firing.

Most navies use some form of close defence systems for last-ditch protection of surface ships. The Goalkeeper system (top and bottom left) is a self-contained CIWS which uses a 30mm rotary cannon, unlike the American Phalanx which has a 20mm weapon. The twin Oerlikon system (top right) requires inputs from the ship's own fire control equipment, while the single 20mm gun (below right) has no fire control apart from a skilled gunner.

Defence against threats from the skies is an ever-present concern on a modern warship. Missiles are responsible for much of this task these days but there is still room for massed fire from small calibre guns. British sailors are shown in the two views on this page, which portray 20mm cannon (left) and hastily fixed general purpose machine guns (below). A heavier punch is possessed by the 76mm twin on the opposite page but this US weapon is virtually obsolete.

Contrasting technology is in evidence here, the view above showing a seaman using a pair of binoculars to maintain a lookout while opposite shows an American sailor in front of screens that form a key part of the Aegis system.

For all the progress that has been made in the development and deployment of "high-tech" weaponry like missiles, room is still set aside for the conventional gun for both defensive and offensive applications. Sadly for battleship aficionados, the era of really heavy firepower is virtually at an end and most modern guns tend to be fairly lightweight, although they are perfectly capable of inflicting quite considerable damage. The guns shown here are a Breda 40mm twin air defence system (above) and two versions of the Creusot 100mm dual purpose weapon.

(Previous page) Of Italian design, the OTO Melara 76mm gun can propel its 14lb (7 kg) shell over a range of almost 10 miles at firing rates which vary from 10 to 85 rounds per minute. In this dramatic study, spent shell cases lie haphazardly in the foreground and it is perhaps not too surprising that this versatile gun has been chosen by nearly 40 of the World's navies.

A long-serving weapon indeed, the acoustic homing torpedo is still employed extensively against targets both on and below the surface. It is also quite a versatile device, in that it may be fired by surface ship or submarine as well as air-delivered by both helicopter and fixed-wing aircraft. The two views at left show seamen readying and firing a torpedo from a deck launcher, whilst the view above depicts an air-delivered torpedo as fitted to a Fleet Air Arm Sea King helicopter.

Although missiles have become ever more widely used aboard the modern warship, there is still room for torpedoes with these long-serving weapons having been much enhanced in recent years. The picture on the left shows a diving team watching intently as deck crew carefully hoist a practice weapon back aboard. On the right US ratings stowing a live torpedo on a destroyer with the aid of what appears to be a rather makeshift type of winch apparatus.

Anti-submarine warfare has been revolutionised since the advent of the helicopter and rotary-wing aircraft are now in widespread naval service around the world. In operation against a sub-surface threat, the homing torpedo is the principal weapon and these pictures are of torpedo-armed helicopters in action. At left is a US Navy Seasprite with the view below showing an Italian Sea King dropping a torpedo upon an unseen target. Lastly, to the right, a Royal Navy Lynx moves off as a torpedo falls seaward, deploying a stabilising parachute.

Asroc (Anti-submarine rocket) is essentially just a Mk.46 acoustic homing torpedo with a "strap-on" rocket booster. Warhead options may vary from conventional explosive to a 1kT nuclear device but the latter is only fitted to US variants. Asroc is seen at left moments after emerging from a Mk.112 eight-round box launcher and above at the moment of detonation.

The latest and most capable helicopter to be deployed on surface warships of the US Navy for the anti-submarine warfare and anti-ship missile defence tasks is the Sikorsky SH-60 Sea Hawk. Seen below in company with its parent ship, the USS *Crommelin*, the Sea Hawk's capabilities allow for a greatly extended search area. The SH-60 is a self-sufficient hunter when it comes to prosecuting a sub-surface threat since it carries its own sonobuoys and other sensors as well as a pair of Mk.46 torpedoes.

Versatility is paramount when it comes to modern naval air power. Westland's Lynx fits the bill nicely, being able to undertake anti-submarine warfare and anti-ship strike duties. In the latter role, it relies on the lightweight Sea Skua missile which is carried and launched by the Royal Navy Lynx seen here.

The largest helicopter type to operate from British ships is the licence-built Westland Sea King, variants now in use including the AEW.3 "radar picket", seen above in close proximity to HMS *Illustrious,* and the HAS.5 shown at left about to "dunk" its sonar. On the opposite page, the cabin area is depicted, with anti-submarine warfare specialists studying displays presenting data generated by the sensors.

The offensive potential of the
Royal Navy's Lynx HAS.1 anti-
submarine helicopter is shown
here, the study at left depicting it
dropping a parachute-retarded
Stingray torpedo as it passes over
the Broadsword class frigate,
HMS Beaver. Above a Mk.45
Torpedo is carried by another
Lynx which also features the
rarely-seen Magnetic Anomaly
Detector device next to the main
undercarriage member.

One of the largest helicopter types to routinely operate from ships at sea, France's SA.321G Super Frelon is able to perform both defensive and offensive missions. Defensive application is shown above by a Super Frelon about to dunk its sonar equipment and hunt for a lurking submarine while offensive potential is seen opposite, where another Super Frelon is portrayed carrying and launching the formidable Exocet sea-skimming radar-guided anti-ship missile.

As has always been the case, warships under way often make splendid subjects for alert photographers and these three portraits certainly convey a feel for both sea and ships. At left, back-lighting cannot disguise the distinctive form of a Ticonderoga cruiser, its stern carrying a single SH-60 helicopter. Below, its flight deck lined with aircraft, is the imposing bulk of the USS *Coral Sea* while the last view depicts a Los Angeles class nuclear-powered submarine as it cruises on the surface at sunset.